UNNECESSARY

ROUGHNESS

Lacresha Hayes

LANICO MEDIA HOUSE
Words that wield power, imagination and life

A division of Lanico Enterprise

Arkansas Texas Louisiana

Unless otherwise noted, all Scripture quotations are from the King James Version of the Bible.

Publisher is Lanico Media House, an imprint of Lanico Enterprise.

Printed in the United States of America

For the man who taught me to stop turning a deaf ear and a blind eye,

who taught me awareness, and who clearly showed me who I am.

Contents

Acknowledgments

There are some people who play the game of football so amazingly well that it gets even a passerby excited. As a teen, my first football love was Dan Marino. He had the most amazing eyes and played the game well. Then the Miami Dolphin colors and the movie, Ace Ventura: Pet Detective, turned me into a diehard fan.

Later, I got caught up in Bo Jackson. Bo knew everything. I wanted to know Bo. Then Deion Sanders came with his flair and I got caught up in his fanfare. But I have never loved anyone as much as I loved Brett Favre.

Because of Brett Favre, I learned enough about the game to write this book. Because of his tenacity and spirit, I decided to tackle a tough subject for me, football, and show how it is a game of relationships.

Lastly, I'd like to acknowledge Raynold Dudley for answering 1001 questions about penalties and plays.

.

Introduction

Relationships seem to be the primary focus of most people. People want healthy, functioning marriages, families, and friendships. But it seems no matter how hard we try, difficulties occur. People we once shared a meal with become our "enemies" and those we never much cared for become our friends. The person we vow our hearts to sometimes become the person who hurts us the most- on purpose- over, and over again. At the same time, the one we look down upon is the one aching to give us the commitment we're begging others for.

This isn't a tell-all book about who did what and when, though it is factual. But the purpose is not to parade my personal relationship troubles before you. The purpose is to heal those who are, like I was, suffering silently, dying daily trying to cover up the pain in their hearts. I'm only going to ask two things of my readers: read this with an open mind and without judgment. If you do that, I can almost certainly guarantee you won't make as many mistakes. What's more is you'll find yourself free mentally and emotionally.

With that being said, let's get into the meaty stuff. Happy reading!

Chapter 1

Goal Line

If you've ever taken a road trip and turned on the wrong exit, you understand how frustrating it is to go however many blocks to get back on the interstate just to travel however many miles back to the right exit. Wrong turns, they happen all the time in driving and also in life. In driving, it's easy to identify where you veered off track. But it isn't always so easy to identify our wrong turns in life. Each decision leads to so many other decisions in rapid succession. It reminds me of the football kick-off. The receiver has to make a major decision or two in a split second: kneel or run, and then which direction to run. Once he has committed to run in whatever direction, the play has to be followed through.

The Bible records in Proverbs that all our ways are right to us. We know why we did this or that. We had some logical or emotional reason at the time. It made sense to us then. But just because a decision makes sense, seems better, offers some benefit we think we need, does not make it a sound or wise decision. And so, in life we make many wrong turns through bad choices. Sometimes, we decide without all the information available to us, further increasing the likelihood of regret later on in life.

I remember in 1991 when I first met the guy I'm going to call my Guy. He was a bad boy, gangbanging in our little town like they did in Compton, CA, his hot hang out when he lived in Cali. Oh, he was every bit the gangster, fighter, and hustler that he proclaimed. I was very young, had a young son already by a married man, and was on the way to becoming a bitter young woman. On the other hand, he was dangerous, exciting, fun and carefree. That presented a new dynamic and I got sucked in like most of the neighborhood.

After a brief year of our secret trysts, it ended. I saw that he wasn't compatible with me. His violent nature was terrifying, but the disrespect he had toward all women was even more disturbing. He was young and rugged, and I was entirely too sensitive. Thus, I left my handsome prince because he hadn't yet learned to be charming, but I guess some ember remained lit for him during our 20 year hiatus.

With the things that caused me to stay away over 20 years ago, it still blows my mind I would end up back with him some 20 years later. And from the very beginning of our second chance, there was reason each day to run away. But my slower adult reflexes, broken reasoning, and my adult fears kept me in it at first. For every reason I could find to run, there was always another reason to stay. The older me feared growing older alone. There was a deep seated fear of dating. In fact, at the start of our relationship, I was just a big knot of fear. My husband had chosen to move on with his life while I was in prison. My son was off at a nice distance and fighting to get his life on track. Soon after, my mom died. For all intents and purposes, I was as alone as I'd ever been and it hurt like hell. There was no one around for me to take care of. There was no one there to take care of me. And coming out of prison with no money and three chronic illnesses, I didn't know what my future held. I only knew that somehow I'd have to survive. I didn't know if my business could be rebuilt. I didn't know if my reputation would survive prison. I wasn't Martha Stewart after all.

All these fears, doubts, and wonderings made me feel desperate. Desperate people almost always make ridiculous decisions.

As a former victim of sexual abuse, I always desired protection. I thought my parents should have provided it, but they were futile in their efforts. So I somehow formed a fixation on wanting a hero-type guy or at the very least a tough guy who would give his life for me. I wanted someone to defend me and protect me. Instead of that desire dying out, it intensified with age and issues. So I found myself attracted at times to a problem rather than a solution. In my effort to find someone to protect me, I more often found those who would further victimize and harm me.

When my Guy and I began seeing each other again, I loved the fact that his presence in my life blocked many others with bad intentions from even coming my way. I liked the fun and excitement. I enjoyed his company. We laughed well together. We played well together. In the beginning, everything was new to me. He opened my eyes to things I wanted to know and things I didn't want to know. His skewed perspective of life was compelling to me. It blew me away to hear the things he said, see the way he lived, almost carefree. He didn't regard age, color or education. About all he did regard was animals, and seeing that gentleness he possessed with animals always amazed me. It was as if he felt a kinship with them. I guess in some ways, I understood that. Animals, after all, had their own means of communication. Animals are not emotionally understood by humans very often. Animals are neglected and mistreated for no real reason. So yes, maybe he did feel as though he understood them.

From the beginning, we had troubled interactions. We were both caustic, reactionary people. We had tempers, though his was much scarier than mine, not because it was any worse, but because I'd been in church long enough to know how to carry myself, how to hide away under the decorum of Christianity. He was a street king and there was no decorum other than never showing weakness. So to him, I appeared a fraud, and I suppose that from a certain perspective I was.

Many times, my heart agreed with his outbursts and true feelings on matters, but my mind which had been affected by the Bible knew those things were wrong. Thus when I did agree, it would start a whole process of agreement, guilt, and then repentance. But for him, he seemed not to have an active conscience. He did what he wanted when he wanted with little regard for anyone, including me. And so, it didn't take long for me to realize I'd made a wrong turn to get emotionally involved with my Guy. And to prove it, he told me one night in the middle of laughter and fun, "I'm not your Mr. Right. I am Mr. Wrong. Don't love me. Just like me a lot." Would to God we would heed warnings that come in that loud and clear, but like many, I didn't think I had a cause for concern. I was just having fun and enjoying his company. I wasn't thinking love and marriage... not at that particular moment. I was good, so I thought. So I jumped in the game and didn't understand it, was ill-equipped, and out of shape. This is where and how it started.

Chapter 2

10 Yard Line

"I don't play games," I hear you saying. I remember saying the same... that is until I actually caught myself playing them.

For the majority of my life, I was not a football fan. I didn't get into any sports really, but there were always those standout sports stars everyone knew. Still, after I met my last husband, I had no choice but to finally brave those football waters and learn something about the game. First lesson: the name of the game.

Football is a game of strategy, strength and speed. You're matched against other competitors who want to move that little oblong ball into the end zone for a score. In addition to that primary objective, their secondary objective is to stop the opposition from doing the same. Get it without giving any up is the name of the football game. Then there is this unspoken rule that runs in the undercurrent... it is the rule of "by any means necessary."

I remember being so lost the first time I sat through a whole football game. The calls were absolutely confusing, all but one: unnecessary roughness. I got it the first time I heard it. I liked that call. It was like a haven in a game of very necessary roughness. It seems that call summed up my life.

Unnecessary roughness was the way I was brought up, the way my relationships seemed to work, the way I felt even God dealt with me. So after the first full sit-through of a football game, I found myself looking forward to following the Green Bay Packers and learning football through their journey toward the championship. I'd briefly witnessed successes for the Cowboys and Dolphins. Now, I would commit to sharing the struggle of a single team to get to the top. It wasn't so much like a relationship when two people commit to getting to the finish line together, knowing that opposition is sure to come. It was life. But it was also a game. Games are fun, right?

I have been to a few games, seen a lot of fans watch the games. Seems someone always leaves on top of the world and someone else leaves disappointed, even to the point of tears. You should witness the Twitter feed when a game ends. The fans of the winners are excited and bragging boldly on the expertise of their chosen team. The fans of the losers are blaming, angry, or discouraged. So before long I realized the game is only fun when you're winning. At least, that's the impression an outsider gets. Well, love games are no different.

My Guy was quite a gamer. I guess in the beginning, it didn't matter because I had no intentions of sticking around very long. He was just a fun distraction to help me get over a particularly difficult time in my life. I didn't care about his money. I didn't care if he had a plan. I didn't care if he knew how to have a relationship or not because I didn't plan to have one with him. In fact, a relationship was not on either one of our minds. We just became what neither one of us wanted from the other, a couple.

In football, you know you're playing a game. The boundaries are clearly defined and you recognize what your objective should be. Unfortunately, in the games we play in life and love, the boundaries are not always so clearly defined, and neither are the objectives. Thus love games have high collateral damage. The pain hurts deeper, the tears flow longer, and the disappointment can lead to life-changing depression.

I suppose we never grow out of that hope to find someone who wouldn't want to live one day without us. Thus immature people fall into the lure of jealous games when that "proof of love" desire hits them. They suppose that jealousy is a sign of love, and so being love starved, they set out to make everyone they meet prove their love by evoking strong emotions. Blindly, they do the things that actually increase the odds of bringing their worst fears of rejection and abandonment to pass. I know. Been there and done that. So in the beginning of our relationship, his jealousy was comforting and mine was suppressed. What a team we were, me every bit him except that he acted out and I suppressed. But truly, there was little difference between us on a fundamental level. And maybe that is how we lasted as long as we did. But games and relationships do not mix. They are definitely oil and water and eventually, you lose everything trying to juggle more than you should have to.

From the beginning, there were other women in his life. He had a thing for white girls, I thought. But what I later discovered was that he had a thing for all women. He was all base nature. If it looked good to him, sounded good, then he'd try it. Yes, he had all the right words coming out of his mouth at first. Like most men in the world, he said he wanted a real woman who wouldn't cheat, wouldn't leave, and wouldn't do drugs. Yet he was living with his girlfriend, occasionally sleeping with several of his ex-girlfriends, and daily in my face acting like he didn't want to be doing any of it. I knew better. I was heartbroken and looking for something to get my mind off of my broken 10 year relationship with my husband. I didn't want anything serious with anyone so he was the perfect candidate, someone I didn't think I could love and definitely wasn't seeking his love. From that perspective, you could say I was playing a game with myself. I thought I was signing up for one thing but it turned out to be a whole different game, different objectives, and an outcome that nearly ruined my life.

It amazes me how often people are secretly willing to share the mate they love. They won't verbalize it but they turn a deaf ear and a blind eye to obvious signs of infidelity. We hear the rumors, see the text messages, see the changing screens on the computer when we walk into the room, see the private phone calls, and experience the pain of being ignored and lied to, but refuse to truly address the issue and resolve it even if it means walking away. No, instead many of us take the easy road and choose to pretend there is no problem. Maybe we justify our staying by assuming all men cheat or all women lie, or by fearfully trying to look into the future to see worse than whom we have already. Perhaps, we force ourselves to focus only on the benefits of the relationship. Whatever we use to pacify ourselves in an unfaithful relationship, we stay. We eventually get quiet and shrink, feeling unloved and unwanted, knowing that somewhere there is another woman/man or two or three or an internet full getting the attention we so wish we could get.

In the beginning, where he slept meant nothing to me. But as we continued in an illicit sexual relationship, things began to change. From the first conversation, in his mind I was his. I was not allowed to deal with other guys longer than a hello, and even a hello to the wrong guy could bring on a fight. But for me, that wasn't a problem because there was no one I wanted to deal with longer than a brief hello. Still, I am an equal opportunity type thinker. If you don't want me in other friendships or relating to men, then you need not think you're going to have female friends either. And not only that, but you must be prepared to be my best friend which means listening and hanging out and communicating and all those other friendship activities. But my Guy wanted to have his cake and eat it too.

Still, I dealt with it for a long time. I remember one particular night my Guy had promised to take me out. I bathed, perfumed, dolled myself up... for nothing. After a couple hour of texts saying he was coming, and several unreturned phone calls, I figured out he wasn't coming and nor was he going to answer his phone for me again. Now these days, there's no way a guy would get a second chance after a situation like that. But at that period of my life, I was already low. I felt old, sick, and abandoned. I'd been to prison, had a horrible criminal history, was overweight, and generally depressed. I was too afraid to brush him off at the time. So when he did show up the next day with a weak excuse, I still hopped in the vehicle with him and hung out like nothing had happened and that was when I began losing "the game." It was then that I showed him it was okay to leave me hanging, disrespect me, and abuse my time and trust. Of course, he was home with his "not quite" girlfriend and I knew that. Yet I allowed myself to be used as a whenever-he-had-nothing-to-do girl. I was losing ground and in danger of a touchback.

Competing Strategies

It may amaze you to know that a financially successful woman deals with all the same issues as a woman who is unemployed or underemployed. Beautiful women are cheated on just as often as those society deems not so attractive. It took me a long time as a woman to finally settle the issue of my worth. And that was the key to my freedom. My problem was not that I wasn't beautiful enough, not smart enough, and not rich enough. Many beautiful women who have outwardly successful lives struggle with their own value and worth. Many intelligent and accomplished women have found themselves victimized by a bad relationship decision. Even those who find a way to make it work, still struggle with questions of esteem and worth.

From the outside looking in, I had it together. But those closest to me knew that my life was falling apart, that I was falling apart. A couple of my friends tried to stage interventions for me. They didn't understand the reason behind all the inner turmoil I wrestled with or the public drama that decorated my life from time to time. To be honest, I didn't understand it either. I was a loving and understanding person. I was kind and tender. Sure, I had my ways, but did they warrant all the drama I endured, particularly in relationships with men?

In football, the game is as much about competing coaching strategies as it is skilled players. An excellent player in the wrong position still cripples the team. It's the same in life, and particularly relationships.

It doesn't matter how wonderful you are if you are out of position. Your value shines when you are placed where you should be. Out of position, you look awkward and clumsy. You become a weak link in a chain that is sure to break due to misuse. When you operate outside your purpose, your weaknesses are exposed and you're subjected to abuse. For this reason in football, not only must the players be skilled, but the coaches must have an eye for natural talent and predispositions. It is the coach's job to position the players and to maximize their training for the chosen position, as well as to know when to call in some back up. Traditionally, we should allow God to coach us in the matters of the heart, but we don't always do that. Sometimes, we're coaching and playing at the same time and missing a wealth of information that could change our level of success in our relationships.

In my case, I was losing before I even began playing. I'd chosen the wrong guy at the wrong time. I'd allowed myself to be sucked in by someone who had no respect for women or people in general. Yet, trying to coach and play at the same time, I didn't see that I'd undertaken a losing battle.

In any relationship, there are potentially competing strategies. Each party defines what they want. They present what they offer. The other party does the same and they either agree with one another and embark upon a relationship journey, or they decline and keep looking. My Guy didn't offer much more than financial support and fun. He was the dangerous bad boy that presented an adventure and I was looking forward to that. I had spent almost 6 years on the brink of death and despair, so an adventure seemed like a nice distraction from all my problems. Still, I wasn't considering the long term. Like an overly confident player who thinks it's okay to let a play pass or grant a head start, I toyed around with the enemy and ended up getting burned.

From day one, he was disrespectful with the terminology he used to describe women. He was cheating when he met me. He cheated while he was with me. And from the beginning of our emotional connection, I was almost always in anguish and fear and paranoia. He was often grouchy with me, often argumentative. Yet I stayed. As harsh and verbally abusive as he was, there was something so huge about any small kindness from an otherwise mean person. It was dang near addictive. I fell right into a trap I thought I was above. I thought I was more emotionally mature than that. I thought I was more aware than to fall into the trap of abuse and neglect. Still, I dug in and fought harder to maintain this relationship than any other before it, never mind the fact that it was the worse relationship I'd ever been in. It was full of unnecessary drama, unnecessary pain. Our relationship was, in essence, unnecessary roughness, a football penalty given for using excessive or brute force while on the field. A five yard penalty, a loss of ground.

Offsides

♥

In the great game of football, sometimes players don't line up correctly. At the line of scrimmage, they find themselves on the opposing players' side of the field. Oh, most times it isn't a blatant thing. Sometimes, it is just a fraction but just that fraction can cause another 5 yard penalty. And who wants to go backwards for lining up incorrectly, for trespassing on the opposite team's designated area.

In love relationships, we often trespass into forbidden territory. While it is nice to believe that love opens every door and window, the fact is that we all come with our own hang ups and issues. We are all flawed individuals. Often, one of those flaws is attempting to fix other people. That's a trespass. You're for sure overstepping your boundaries when you take it upon yourself to change someone else. Further, you are about to break your own heart and fill your life with disappointment.

I remember that day that I looked across the car to see "potential" in my Guy. He made a sarcastic joke, and I realized there was a lot of hidden intelligence in him. Yes, he stuttered. He often pretended he couldn't read. He made fun of his "dumbness" on a daily basis. But in one unguarded moment, I saw through the act. I saw a man who felt misunderstood, who'd lived a rough life and had emotional scars that made him feel more comfortable pretending he was stupid.

The day I saw potential was also the day I found myself offsides. I began imagining how things could be if he stopped hiding behind the hustler mentality, released the anger and violence that came so easily to him, and embraced GOD completely. With that beautiful picture in my mind, I proceeded to set a plan in motion to change this current raw material into my dream guy. I began trying to enhance the beauty of God and distract him from the lure of sin. Saying it didn't work out as I planned is a major understatement. In fact, it backfired! He perceived it all as if I thought those who profess Christ were superior to others who did not. The more I tugged at him, the more he rebelled and soon, I lost sight of what I'd seen in the first place. I lost sight of what I was fighting for. I stopped planning and starting reacting to everything, small and large. The leader he was became the symbol of what I stood against. Indeed, he glorified nearly everything I detested... though I was not necessarily innocent of them all, but that's another story.

I was venturing into forbidden territory which leads me to a passing question and thought. What is witchcraft if it is not manipulating another person's will and desires? I was a marketing expert, a book writer, a creative soul. I used that creativity, those wiles, to try to "make" him see Christ was the only right way. But as I ventured into the NO GO zone, I found I was changing. Faced with frustration because of his failure to see it my way, I became bitter and angry. I didn't understand why it was so hard to get him to embrace Christ and become my knight in the kingdom, my holy covering. I could say I was deluded, but yet again, that would be a gross understatement. I was being a damned fool, not cussing but literally using the word damned to say I was headed nowhere but toward my own destruction.

The thing about trespassing is you put yourself in danger. According to the law of the land, when you trespass, you may be harmed. Things are no different in the other realms either. When you trespass into someone's soulish realm, meaning you overstep your bounds to try to control or influence their mind, will and emotions, you are playing God. And since you aren't God, you will find yourself frustrated and in danger of losing yourself trying to save someone else.

As I saw the rebellion against my attempts to save him, to transform him into someone better, I began to question God and question myself. That, my friends, was the best part of the situation because that 5 yard penalty called offsides actually catapulted me in spiritual wisdom and understanding. There is nothing like a penalty to get your attention and teach you a lesson.

Chapter 3

20 Yard Line

When football starts, the ball is kicked off. If the player catches it in the end zone, he can kneel and the next play will start at the 20 yard line automatically. Now if the player thinks it is clear for him to run it further, he will make a go for more yards. Often times, in the pros, you'll see the player kneel. So many first downs begin on the 20 yard line.

Brett Favre was known as the gunslinger. That man had an amazing arm on him as a quarterback. He was tough as nails too. He could hustle. He could hit a target on the move in nearly any direction. However, almost every team understood that and would keep the pressure on Brett. This caused him to throw a lot of interceptions too. He was sacked often. One day while the Packers lined up on the 20 yard line, the announcers were discussing Brett's NFL record. He had a lot of interceptions but also a lot of passing yards. We sat there discussing whether he would pass or use a run play. Of course, he passed it and hit his target. The first play of the game was a success and resulted in a gain in yards.

In relationships, the first play of the game happens in a less profound way. Most times, they sort of evolve from hanging out and spending time on the phone or internet together. So because there is often no whistle like in basketball, it can be hard to discern when a relationship begins. Are we friends? Are we dating? Basically like in football, you're waiting for the hike. You're waiting for the cue to get the show on the road.

Facemask

I think it is interesting that in the game of football, they do not allow you to grab and handle people by their facemask. It'll earn you yet another penalty. However, thinking logically, those helmets are on for protection and those masks sit out from the face to offer protection to one of the more sensitive areas of the body. So while each player *wants* to protect his face in such a rough game, it is quite easy to overstep the boundary and find your hand tied up in another player's mask.

From a relationship perspective, we often use masks to protect ourselves. We want to be loved for the person we are under that mask, but we don't want anyone forcefully unmasking us. We want to unmask when we're ready, when the game is over, when we think we're safe. How much like football is a relationship?

During courtship, most people present each other with facemasks. On rare occasions, the real person peeks out. Reminiscent of a turtle, many people present themselves a little at a time, especially those who have been hurt. It's a side effect of heart pain often times.

In my relationship during different times while he was intoxicated, I caught glimpses of a tenderhearted man who'd been hurt and disappointed so much that it now hurt to believe in goodness again, though he desired it so much. Each time I saw that, I fought desperately to hold on to it. I guess in essence I was attempting to remove his facemask during game time, a huge penalty. And like in the great game of football, each time I tried, I suffered tremendous loss.

There is nothing wrong with your desire to be loved as you are, emotionally, spiritually and physically naked. And when you love someone, often you desire to know them deeper, more intimately. However, you cannot force that kind of love or intimacy. You cannot beg upon it. You cannot manipulate someone into it. You must simply wait for such a love. It has to be given of freewill and it will not happen during game time. It is only in a moment of safety that any of us will unmask ourselves. It is in a place of no games, no perceived threat, and acceptance that we relax our defenses enough to be truly seen.

Here, I need to interject something important. The game of football is not a game of love, nor was it designed for any kind of intimacy or kindness. It is a dog-eat-dog, survival of the fittest type of game. Weaknesses are quickly exploited, both on and off the field. A professional football player is a football player in season and out, at work and at home. He is not allowed to do anything that might damage his value as a player. Literally, he has to sell all the way out to the game or he will not survive long.

The games we play in relationships are the same. They block intimacy and don't allow for true kindness or love. Instead of building both parties into a unit, games divide couples and pit them as opposites and competitors. Both parties want the same thing but refuse to work together because they are blinded by the faulty programming of the world. They do not trust each other enough to put all the cards on the table, so it becomes a game to discover what is in the mind and heart of the other. I think that's terribly sad, but it happens every day. Tons of potentially wonderful relationships are ruined by games, having their wings clipped before they learn to fly.

Sacked

I think it goes without saying that no quarterback wants to be sacked. It's a loss of yards and can potentially be dangerous. There have been stories of teams purposefully taking the star quarterback of the opposing team out with an injury. If an opponent makes it to the quarterback, the objective is to take him down hard before he can throw that ball. If he tries to run with the ball, then take him down even harder.

At the start of watching football games, I was instantly a Brett Favre fan. Still, everyone who has seen him play knows that he has endured his share of sacks because he would hold the ball until what he wanted opened. When it worked, he was seen as a genius, but when it didn't, he was deemed old, out of step and foolish. Anyway, a sack takes you back. And who wants to be forced backward?

In relationships, things aren't much different. When we engage in a game with our significant other, we go backwards and sometimes without even being aware. The lies and manipulation cannot produce forward progress. The cheating and mistreating are not forward progress. They take you further from your goal of love and dedication. You cannot do all the wrong things and expect to go forward, not in football and not in life.

The primary reason most quarterbacks are sacked is holding the ball too long without moving around, or shuffling. In my relationship, I made the same mistake. I was trying to hold on to my heart, but I wasn't shuffling. I was standing in one spot, an easy target for the picking. So foolish was I to try to have a relationship without a real investment of my heart. Truth is, if you cannot release your heart in a relationship, you certainly don't need to stay in it.

Now, when pressure comes on a quarterback, either he has to trust and release the ball, or he has to get out of the pocket and protect the ball himself. But what he should never do is stand around waiting for the sack. Of course, many of us have made that terrible decision, the decision not to commit but stay in the relationship.

Another reason quarterbacks are sacked is because they lack protection. The player who is supposed to support his blindside is distracted or otherwise detained and unable to cover his QB. When that happens, a hole is opened that leaves the QB vulnerable, and the defense takes full advantage of the opening. In this tough as nails game, each party has a role and when one person falls short of their role or proves unable to fulfill it due to the opposition coming on too strong, the whole team suffers. Doesn't that sound just like a relationship? It does to me.

I remember the beginning when my Guy used to tell me stories about things he'd seen and done in his youth. He was all smiles while he told stories about cheating, getting caught, fighting and slapping on his women, and running from the police. He basically enjoyed everything I found reprehensible. I looked back upon some of my stories with disgust, but he looked at those same kinds of stories in his life as good memories and pleasant flashbacks. Yet he couldn't stand to hear one of my stories from my youth.

The things I knew about him first hand and the things he told me made me afraid to invest anything in him. I didn't want to tie my heart to someone so foul at the core, which is how I judged him for the majority of our relationship. Thus, I felt the pressure of wanting what I wanted, which was a committed marriage relationship and yet I was in a relationship that had no promise of such. There was pressure to leave and pressure to stay. So like my beloved Brett Favre has done many times, I froze in the pocket and received a lot of damage because of it. Getting sacked almost cost me my career, my sanity and my freedom, if not my life. I guess you could say, I'd been bagged and tagged because I definitely wasn't alive in the relationship. I was all stimuli and reactions. Namely, I was either angry or paranoid throughout the entire relationship. I didn't trust the laughs, the plans, the "good" times. I was always waiting on the next argument, next fight, or next lie.

Now before you think I'm bashing my Guy, this book is really about me taking the hard path to a destination that had many easier roads. It is me showing how perspective is everything. Blaming takes power out of your hands and mine. So even when he lied, cheated, hit or disrespected me, the responsibility to end that behavior was mine. I chose rather to try to fix him, change him or train him. All of those were colossal wastes of time. Only fools think that they have the power to change another individual at will when our own changes do not come so easily.

During this seemingly endless struggle, I finally learned the cause of most relational frustrations, rather in friendships or intimate relationships. We walk into the relationship hoping to mold someone else into who we think they should be, the person we want. Do you hear how selfish that sounds? To want to mold someone into what we think they should be is to say who they are now isn't good enough. How absolutely devastating to a relationship for that to be a reality! Moreover, it takes way less energy to select the one who suits us in the first place than to grab whoever is available and try to change their personality and character. All of this is a step backward, and I was sprinting backwards while seemingly walking in my heightened sense of awareness. What a joke!

Before I move on from this topic, let me bring up another interesting point about being sacked in football. When the QB is sacked, on the next down, he has to make up for the lost yards. Many times, it puts the offensive team in a crunch time situation, though on some occasions, it is the fire needed to spur a powerful run, an amazing throw, or a comeback touchdown. Sometimes, going backwards is how we get what we need to get ahead. Because of the pain of loss and the desperation not to lose, we open ourselves to possibilities we were once closed to.

After my Guy and I had been together for a while, God began to deal with me. Every time I was angry with him, I'd talk to God about it without much of an answer or any comfort in the beginning. Time passed yet there was no improvement in my mental and emotional state. I was still undecided, completely double-minded about our relationship. I was emotionally unstable. I was in a pretty bad condition, spiritually, mentally and emotionally. Yet, God is faithful and merciful and He began dealing with me, heart first. I could argue with people who tried to peel me, but when God began peeling me in our somewhat distant relationship, pulling me closer by pulling off the layers of protective gear I donned, I could no longer argue. I had to humble myself and accept what I was being shown.

As God showed me my own insecurities, my character weaknesses and fears, I realized that it wasn't all bad. For months, my prayers had been based upon a victim mentality. It wasn't based upon truth. It wasn't centered in faith. I was praying my fears and walking blindly. But it wasn't until I took a few steps back and suffered some loss that I could comprehend these things.

Before my great fall, I didn't know that I was so fearful, so hateful, so judgmental, so hypocritical, or so lost. I was walking in the power of God concerning others but not myself and that's the deepest sadness. So in this "relationship from hell" as others termed it, I found a closer, more personal walk with God, a freedom that I'd never known. Losing yards made me desperate enough to seek the answer from the ANSWER and to accept whatever He spoke. So, while no one wants to be sacked, if you find yourself in that position right now, stop crying and begging for it to end.

Decide to see, hear, and feel it all. Decide to learn, to grow even in the thickest mud. Be that lotus flower that grows in the mire.

It doesn't matter how those around you see you while you're struggling. What does matter is that you continue to make progress toward wholeness. Oftentimes, when a QB is sacked, emotionally he has two choices: be down and ashamed, even angry or be determined not to let that foil the team's plan for a touchdown. Same for you, is this sack going to make you bitter or will you let it make you better?

Chapter 4

30 Yard Line

As my Guy and I continued to waste time and vacillate between making it work or hanging on until something better came along, things began to get serious, even dangerous. We began to have severe arguments that led to physical fights. Several times, I found myself nursing bruises and one time bad enough to warrant a visit to the hospital. It was hard to believe I was back in that place after preaching to thousands of women about securing their safety and trusting God enough to walk away. Now, I was back in an abusive situation myself and either I had to walk the talk or stop talking the talk. It was a hard shift that required an immediate decision since almost all of our arguments somehow ended up on Facebook, where I'd built my coaching career.

I was growing in online and offline popularity. My gifts were making room for me and in some places, I was becoming like a household name. My social media influence was well over 10 million individual users. For a little Arkansas girl who quit school, got a GED, went to college but never could seem to finish, that was an amazing accomplishment. Yet I wasn't happy because I wasn't trying. I wasn't maxed out. My potential called for so much more. I kept thinking my boyfriend was slowing me down, hindering my growth, acting as a distraction to my destiny. But in truth, he was doing none of those things.

It wasn't him who chose to demote God in my life. It wasn't him who was trying to live two lives. He had one life, and he lived it in public and in private. I was the one trying to blend two lives that could not be blended, that should not be blended.

Fumble

When a football player catches the ball and brings it in, he can run with it. But if the player never brings the ball under his control, it eventually falls to the ground and a fumble is called. A fumble is simply dropping the ball. How many times have we dropped the ball in life? In relationships?

I've seen football games in which the ball was passed and as the player went up to catch the ball, another player was upon him and tackled him, causing the ball to come loose, to come out of his control. When that happens, the ball is still live until someone controls it. Whichever team is able to fall directly on the ball, who has hands directly on that ball will control it the next play of the game.

If you look at most relationships, the goals are love and companionship. There are so many times when we think we've found them. Yet it seems that as soon as we put our hands on it to wrap them around our relationship goals, it slips right through our fingers. We fumble love, companionship, trust, commitment and promise. Maybe from game weariness, from lack of knowledge, from outside interference, whatever the reason, we lose our grip at the wrong time. We thought we had it under control just to look up and find a mountain of trials trying to fall on top of it. Seems life itself is the cruelest when it comes to love. The one we love already loves someone else. The one they love may be with them but may not be completely invested. So many broken relationships because everyone is busy trying to force someone to give them what they want rather than going out and finding someone who is already free and offering the things desired.

Impatience causes some men and women to go through entirely too many bedmates, soul ties and heart aches seeking love, companionship, understanding and commitment. Somehow, many of us have embraced the lie that we can teach a person to love us. The issue is, the only person who can learn to love is one who is willing to learn it, one who has decided on their own to love. It cannot be forced or coerced. In a healthy and proper relationship, we can voice our opinions, needs and issues and work through it together. But if you wake up and find yourself in one in which your opinions and thoughts are not valued and your voice is not heard, then there is nothing more to be done. At that point, you must release it to God and make some tough decisions. Fault-finding, manipulation and guilt-trips will not work.

In our relationship, I guess you could say I was one of those players who fumbled. The referee blew the whistle and threw the flag but I was reacting and fighting to hold on to something I'd already lost. The referee was God. He had to remake my self-image, train my thinking and flush me of the fear I'd lived with all my life. Not once did God deal with me about what was wrong with my boyfriend. Contrary to popular opinion, God isn't angry with sinners when they sin. He understands that we are but dirt without His precious breath. A sinner cannot help but to sin. For all the angry God preaching we hear, God is not an angry God. He's not a vengeful God either. He's not up there thinking, "Oh, that's my favorite right there and I'm going to strike everyone who hurts her." While it feels comforting to hear those words, it isn't the truth. I always knew that but during our relationship, I learned so much more about God's long suffering love.

One of the first lessons I learned as our love continued to suffer fumbles is that it is not my right to force my will upon anyone else. Our dominion as believers begins and ends with us and those who choose to fall under it. Our freewill is never more important than someone else's, our desires are not to be realized by sacrificing and manipulating others. And in love relationships, people often, even without realizing it, try to manipulate the other into the position that makes them most comfortable. But at the point of submission to the other's will, the relationship loses the balance and fullness of the characteristics of both parties. It becomes unbalanced because, essentially, the stronger one is now only in relationship with him/herself since they have manipulated the weaker party into submitting every characteristic that chaffed or challenged them. I love myself, but I truly don't want another me. It wouldn't work long. Still, if I begin working on my mate trying to iron out the wrinkles I see, trying to reprogram him into what I believe in, I'm in essence creating a one-sided relationship.

I remember packing up all my things and leaving a couple of times, thinking that things couldn't get any worse and that I couldn't handle it another day, but each time I ended up back at home with him. I went back after the fights. I went back after the lies and philandering. I stayed through the name-calling, the online date sites and the constant stalking activity of ex-girlfriends. In fact, everything that a man could do to a woman he did to me and I stayed. It couldn't be love that caused it. Love doesn't quite work that way, though you'll probably read that in a million books. Truth is, those kind of battles only happen when one person tries to force another to change, to adapt, or into submission. Love does not force its own will. Love does not seek his own way. Love sees the heart and need and releases the adored person to be who he/she wants to be without restrictions. So had it been love, I would have simply released him to continue on being the person he enjoyed being. I wouldn't have tried to guilt him into change or control his activities to stop him from doing the things that hurt me so much.

My Guy and I were bound together in fear. We were both afraid to let go, and that fear was unexplainable. We both knew we could move on and find someone else, for better or worse. We'd been in relationships before and would again, but somehow an invisible bond was formed in dangerous jealousy and unrealistic fear. God began doing open heart surgery on me, beginning with my fears.

During this time, a strategically placed sister, Armetria Charles, began working with me about some things through a little bit of personal coaching. This woman teaches powerfully on fear and love and securing your own relationship with God. As my friend, she popped into my life right on time. In fact, after our first full conversation in which she ministered to me, I found myself under arrest less than an hour later. That may not sound compelling but she only asked me one question during the ministering: "Lacresha, where do you feel closest to God, when He ministers to you the most?" Guess what my answer was. If you said jail, you're right. Within an hour of making that declaration, I was arrested for a 10 year old warrant for old fines. I spent 26 days in jail, time spent in reflection and prayer.

Armetria's short plea played in my head and heart as soon as I was arrested. We've had a nick of time friendship ever since. Her plea: "Lacresha, release your fear. There is no lack in you. You don't need all the things and people you are afraid to be without."

When I was arrested, immediately my Guy disappeared. I called him 12 times over 2 hours before I finally got him on the phone though he was sitting right beside me when I got arrested. I had never felt more abandoned, or more hurt. I couldn't imagine what would make a man who loves you not answer the phone when you needed him most. So my first week in jail was all blame, fear and nerve endings. Bad dreams plagued me at night so that even my sleep held no pleasure or reprieve.

During those days in jail, I discovered how useless and tormenting fear truly is. I also discovered a lot more about relationships. For instance, I didn't know and couldn't know what he was doing, and whatever he was doing, it was not physically harmful to me, didn't change one fact of my life and thus, it wasn't really important. The freedom I experienced when that first lesson set in was indescribable!

If you're wise, a fumble will teach you some amazing things. It can actually save you from further trouble and embarrassment. But if you choose not to learn from your mistake, this fumble will be just another in a long line of them. At some point, you have to decide to grow from every happening in your life. Don't let one pain or disappointment be wasted.

Chapter 5

40 Yard Line

Game progress is important because there is only so much time available. The offensive team needs to move the ball down the field and into the end zone. The only time a team benefits from slowing the game down is during the last minutes when a score could cause the leading team to lose the game. In that case, the leading team tries to hold the ball as long as possible. But during the first three quarters, that is not the case.

I was in a rush to get somewhere I hadn't defined. Half the time, I didn't even know which direction I was going. One moment I wanted this and the other moment something different. Completely double-minded, I blamed my ex for every flaw he possessed but it was not him stopping our forward progress as much as it was me. I was only half sure I wanted to be with him most days. Some days passed with us feeling stuck together. Other days, we were only moments from splitting. But then there were those days when we vibed and his ridiculousness was hilarious and my griping was comforting. I think the majority of our days passed in mundane activity, trying to pacify our discontent with various aspects of our lives, especially our financial situation.

As with anything, no matter how hard you try, there are times when outside influence and inner troubles collide to throw you into a tailspin. In the beloved game of football, I can think of two such instances: the pass interference and the incomplete pass.

Pass Interference

♡

The interesting thing about this call to me is that the whole game seems like it could qualify for some type of interference. I mean, the QB has people after him as soon as the ball is hiked. Each offensive player streaking down the field has someone streaking with them to stop them from making the catch, or to tackle them as soon as they do. There's a match on the defense for every player on the offense and their job is to make scoring impossible. They are basically professional interferers.

Still with pass interference, the defensive team is penalized for being overzealous and getting in the way before the appropriate time. As rough as the game is, there are still rules and penalties for breaking them... so much like relationships.

Many times in my life, I found someone who I cared for, wanted and dated just to find troubles caused by outside interference. His family or mine, our friends or exes, in every relationship there was someone causing problems. It took a very long time for me to discover the secret to overcoming interference because it cannot always be avoided.

One day during a particularly emotional game, I was upset because Brett Favre was being roughed up and sacked and hurt, purposefully in my opinion. After a couple of pass interference calls, finally Brett let them run the ball. That was a good call and landed the Vikings a touchdown after a few more plays. Well, I learned a valuable lesson with that game: if what you're doing isn't working, if your opponent seems to have your number, then do something different. Explore other options. Run a different play.

As a public figure, though by no means a superstar, I live a fairly open life, flaws and all. I refuse to have to apologize for being human so I decided to never pick up that hypocritical mask to make others think I've arrived. I'm on the journey along with the next person. But when my Guy and I became an item, it created a social media frenzy. The preacher was with the drug dealer. The lady was with the tramp. The woman of God had bedded down with the devil. It was hilarious that people made such a big deal out of it, and frankly, if they hadn't, our relationship probably would not have lasted so long. Oh and believe me, things were no different for him.

From the beginning, people in his family and his buddies would tell him that I was crazy, jealous, psychotic, a hater, and the term that everyone seemed to love, a bitch. I was always accused of sleeping with everybody but no one could give everybody a name. I was accused of working voodoo and witchcraft, which is also hilariously ridiculous! To them, I was an enigma. No one knew quite what to think of me and yet people told him what to think of me all the time. He tried to filter his responses to me through the things people had said. Problem was, he didn't even realize he was doing it.

From the beginning, he saw me as a liar, a thief, a con artist, and a whore. I just happened to be cute and had a nice body, which distracted him from the things that ran through his mind about me. In his eyes, there was no way I was as "perfect" as I pretended to be. Of course, I never pretended to be perfect. But the character, the respect and the decency he saw in me he refused to believe for years. So with every argument, I was a "nasty, dirty ass bitch" and worthless.

It hurt to hear other people talking through him. Half of it was his past relationships and pains, but the other half was the talk of the town streets, streets I hadn't truly seen in 17 years. But if you let them tell it, they knew me like the back of their hands. I was a money-hungry, conniving, gold-digging danger to all men and the women who loved them. Nothing could have been further from the truth, but the time wasted trying to convince someone of your innocence is time that yields no reward and no return. Over the years, I continued to wait on a quiet time, a period of peace with him, but it never came. If one person wasn't kicking up dirt, then someone else was. From fake Facebook profiles set up just to hurt us to private phone calls and a slew of text messages, the interference would not cease. So we were always at war within and at war without. I was fighting for love and respect in the relationship and fighting for my right to decide who I want to be with outside the relationship. With one breath, I defended a relationship with him that in the next breath I myself despised. I mean, what was I really fighting to protect? Was I going to keep defending us when he was doing me the most damage?

One of the biggest lessons in life is that the human heart has a huge capacity for forgiveness when we want to forgive and allow it to happen. It can happen not only for the person you love, but the people you don't care for who bring drama and confusion into your life. Sometimes, when every direction you try to take is blocked somehow, you learn to be still and pay attention. You learn to explore out of the box options. You learn or you die in frustration.

Because all roads out of the relationship seemed blocked, several times when I really wanted to be done, I found myself forced to be still, be quiet and let God teach me something through my Guy. He was like the professor of forgiveness and understanding in my life. The more people tried to pressure us apart, the more it seemed God whispered for my stillness.

I think the icing on the cake was the night his ex hacked his Facebook page and posted her pictures with adoring statements. The whole time, before that night, I used to believe most of the stuff she texted me or told me on the phone. After being in his presence all day long, answering his phone all day for him, I knew that the stuff she was saying was a lie, and I realized I had become reactionary in the relationship. I allowed others to pull my strings too much. But that night, I made a vow to myself to tune others out of my relationship. Things are hard enough for a couple when no one interferes with lies or the truth. But trying to have a citywide relationship is certainly not a wise decision. A relationship is between two people, not three, ten or a thousand, or in our case, social media.

In football, a pass or hand off is between two people. The QB has to get the ball into the hands of the receiver or runner. If anyone else gets in between that, it causes problems and can result in the play being aborted, if not the ball being turned over to the opposing team. It stops forward progress. And just like football, in a relationship, letting others in between muddies the water and can cause miscommunication and a failure for the relationship to thrive.

Incomplete Pass

What is the purpose of a pass? To transfer the ball and move it down the field. In football, it's hard to lose sight of the ball because the whole game is centered around it, however, the ball isn't always easily seen in all the commotion on the field. Now in relationships, we pass our love. Sometimes, we lose sight of what we're supposed to be passing because of interference, because of ignorance, or sometimes both. Sometimes, we send out the wrong signals. Sometimes, the receiver incorrectly interprets our signals. Either way, it results in a missed opportunity to score or move ahead.

The funny thing about this call in the game of football is how common it is, so much so that people come to expect it. Sometimes, the QB is forced to throw the ball away rather than take a sack. Sometimes, the receiver is covered and unable to catch the ball. But I think the hardest to watch are the ones when the QB lays the ball right into the hands of the receiver just to have it slip through his fingers for no apparent reason. Clumsy fingers and weariness has broken many a football fans' hearts. Imagine the emotional trauma done when we miss messages and assume motives in relationships.

As my relationship progressed with my Guy, I realized we had genuine concern and care for one another, at least at times. Nevertheless, we had a breakdown in communication when it came to relaying those feelings. Speaking for myself, I think I did mostly know how he felt for me, but I also could see the ebb and flow of interest and disinterest that always threw me for a loop. I was totally insecure in the relationship, too sensitive and reactionary.

In most relationships, we try to love in a way that we think we want to be loved. We try to give what we have been taught, but rarely do we take time and ask someone to teach us how to love them. Yet that is how an incomplete love pass is avoided, by learning the play with the person you're actually planning to pass to. I guess that is why professional athletes are often penalized for missing practice. Practice is necessary to perfect a play.

In relationships, learning your plays with the partner you plan to keep playing with is imperative. Many people can teach you many things about love and relationships, but no one can teach as well as your mate, since that is the object of your love after all.

Often times, we run practice with different people and expect that at game time, things are going to go lovely even though we're paired with someone else. That is usually the foundation of miscommunication. You're speaking. Your mate is speaking, but neither of you are speaking the other's language. After all the trials and problems, you're both tired and suffering from emotional wounds, causing both of you to sometimes even miss the obvious. The call- incomplete pass.

Chapter 6

50 Yard Line

The fifty is the halfway mark for both teams. If you've managed to keep the ball and move it up the field to the fifty, you may be a little more confident, like the end is in sight. However, the opposing team is a little more pressured and desperate to stop you. So things will intensify. One party full of expectation and one full of determination.

In a relationship, your halfway mark is often the place where you both decide to go the distance together, the place of a heart commitment. It happens before marriage but after the courtship has been operating for some time. It is that place where the newness has dulled and reality of building together is setting in. That's our relationship 50.

Turnover on Downs

As I learn more about football, I find the worst case scenario for an offensive team is a turnover on downs in the opposite team's end zone. When a team loses the ball to the opponent's control, not only did they miss an opportunity to score, but now they run the risk of the opponent scoring. If the team was already behind, their chances of losing the game increase dramatically each time they have a turnover on downs.

The goal of a relationship is love and unity, intimacy. Each person desires a mate who will cherish them, assist them and support them. End goal, a long-lasting and happy marriage. When games get involved, goals often shift. Suddenly, instead of seeking love given by freewill, we seek to own, control and manipulate others. It is a symptom of not knowing our value or not trusting others to be able to love us. Either way, we begin to play with our partners. We basically put them on trial and begin simulating events to test the boundaries of their feelings and reactions. We play up the good and even fabricate a bit, go along with what is said even when we secretly don't agree, and adopt ways that seem to please the people we desire. In the end, though, those perfectly woven webs turn out to be traps for us and for our relationships. Because once our own feelings are involved, suddenly we feel cheated, like we cannot be ourselves or are not accepted as we are. Usually the last thought or consideration is what we've done to ensnare ourselves.

In my relationship with my Guy, I did what many of us do. I smiled on cue. I laughed at what he called jokes, even if I did find them crude or reprehensible. I listened to his music, though most of it I didn't personally care for. I even learned to adore his favorite hobby, smoking weed. I reinvented myself, but that was to my own undoing. It wasn't that he asked me to make these concessions. It was that I falsely believed that was how you dated, adoring, and pretending to adore when you couldn't adore. I mean, from children we learn this prehistoric form of witchcraft and manipulation. It begins with a soft tone, with the occasional wiles used to sway decisions.

You see your parents "turn on the charm" for one another, bringing smiles and pleasure. You hear the tone differences, see the flirty actions when something is desired. You learn that charm can get you places and win favor with the right people. But charm is deceptive. It is a temporary yielding of opinion and personality to get past someone's guards, to get what we want.

As I went out of my way to win favor with my Guy, I didn't realize I was losing ground. Every down, I was failing to progress the ball. I looked the part. I talked the part. I walked the part. But no matter how much I looked it, talked it and walked it, I was not IT. I wasn't truly that woman I pretended to be. The fact that I was the one under pressure to pretend is proof enough I was going backward, but I didn't see it in the beginning.

Day by day, I was losing touch with my purpose, losing sensitively to the Spirit, losing sight of what I'd already accomplished and most of all, losing my grip on my own identity. Faking has a way of doing that to you. I styled my hair differently. I ate foods I wasn't especially fond of. I spoke in ways I couldn't believe. I was transforming myself to win something the real me couldn't deal with or maintain. Close friends tried to tell me that, but I didn't comprehend it then. Or rather, I didn't want to hear it at the time. I knew they were right, but I was determined to prove them and myself wrong. Mind games, they always start at home. We're always our own first victim, always our own worst victimizer.

Thinking I was in control, I played with my own soul and my destiny and all my dreams to be with this man. He didn't request it or require it. I cannot at all blame him. It was faulty programming and desperation at the thought of growing old alone. I was afraid that I was running out of time to build this dream marriage I'd always wanted. The older I got, the more forceful I became about this dream of mine of being insanely happy in a romantic marriage. So with him, even though I knew we weren't on the same wavelength, I was determined to remake him for my purpose, but the only person who was changing was me.

It was a turnover on downs. Not only did he have control of the ball, but he was moving it down the field at lightning speed. My defenses were helpless, not because he was so great at the game, but because I was discombobulated. I'd trespassed into a no-go zone. My defensive team had no rest, no preparation and a losing strategy. The offense wasn't scoring, and the defense wasn't defending. I was in trouble!

Chapter 7

The Blitz

In football, when the passer or QB is making some great plays, sometimes the defense will call for a blitz, or an attack on the passer. This call brings on a sudden flurry of rushing defensive players who are out to stop the QB. It is hard for an inexperienced or unsuspecting offense to counter a blitz. For a losing defensive team, a blitz has the potential to turn the game around, putting excessive pressure on the quarterback to perform quickly over and over again.

When I started writing this book, I was still in my broken relationship. In fact, it was through writing this book that I wrote myself free from the bondage of a losing emotional investment. In fact, I was in the middle of an all-out blitz when I sat down and began sharing my story.

My Guy and I could not get along. We were arguing and fighting constantly. My finances were in the pit. My bills were overdue. I'd lost my last parent. My son was gone and independent, but needed help I couldn't offer. I had no car and was barely able to keep a roof over my head. I was fighting and being arrested and charged with felony after felony. I was smoking weed, drinking every few weekends, and still grieving over my broken marriage. I was in no shape to be on the playing field, but there I was- suited up and trying to play with major injuries. Life had blitzed me. I could feel the pressure.

It's a funny thing that happens inside many of us. When we're at our lowest, we also crave love and affection more intensely. But when we are most desperate for love is the worst time to actually try to find it. Oftentimes, the pressure we are feeling on the inside is transferred to the person we finally fixate upon. That pressure squeezes the life out of the relationship and leaves a bitter taste in each party's mouth.

When you're struggling emotionally, physically, spiritually and financially, it increases the pressure on your relationship to perform. It is so easy to transfer that pressure to your significant other, trying to make them be your happiness, be your joy, be your answer, pressure for them to rescue you. If you've never heard it, pressure can bust a pipe, and it is certainly harmful in romantic and platonic relationships.

I remember when Brett Favre played for the Green Bay Packers and Aaron Rodgers was his back up in training. Favre is a legend. Now he's thrown a ton of interceptions, but for a long time, he had more passing yards than anyone else. Rodgers had some huge shoes to fill. That's pressure. When Rodgers began playing after Favre left, I saw a lot of blitzing going on, but somehow over the course of his first year or two, he worked it out and solidified his own spot as a QB. He showed that he was to be taken seriously. He was under pressure to perform and the pressure to continue on after a legend. I'm sure it couldn't have been easy to be Rodgers, but with courage, he stepped up to the plate and led the team to some amazing victories.

When defensive players bring on the blitz, the offense's weaknesses are exposed. That is when the rubber meets the road for many. Same in relationships. When the pressure comes, the truth of what you have built with someone else is exposed. Character is exposed. Intentions are exposed. Exposure can be uncomfortable and even painful, but it can also bring about healing. In my case, I used the pain of exposure to address those hidden issues of my heart, and those unresolved issues from my childhood. I had to face some of my closeted skeletons and put some things to rest permanently. Primarily though, it was fear I had to put to rest because fear and love cannot co-exist or rule together. One is going to overcome the other.

Fear had ruled in my life and relationships, not just with my Guy, but period, even in my broken marriages. But when the pressure built up to an explosion, and I stabbed my ex, I knew something had to change because I was risking everything I loved for something I was only half sure I wanted. I was making illogical choices. I was reacting. I wasn't thinking, truly praying, or yielding to the creative Spirit of God within. I was slave to fear, slave to pain, and slave to broken reasoning.

It was an all-out blitz against, not my relationship, but my purpose and my peace. You see, when you fixate upon the relationship, you lose sight of the true goal of life. Yes, the goals of a relationship are commitment and intimacy and unity and love. But the goal of life is more than just a relationship. The goal of any life should be to live productively, honorably and to have peace and joy while being in communion with the Holy Spirit. When the smaller extracurricular interferes with the purpose of the whole, then the smaller has to removed or rectified. In other words, don't let your relationship or a desire for one cause you to dishonor who you are (identity) and why you are (purpose). Keep your identity and purpose always firmly in sight and let it guide all your decisions, especially those of the relationship sort.

Roughing the Passer

During a blitz, the passer is roughed up, excessively sometimes. It seems when defensive players get their hands on the QB, they try to do the most damage possible. So sometimes, even when the play is over, there will be a late hit or an extra push and shove. They want the QB off his game because no play happens without him, other than a field goal. So to disable the passer is to cripple the offense severely. Therefore, yet another penalty call was created to protect him: roughing the passer.

In football as in life, we have to protect our star player. Many thousands of relationships fail because those involved treat each other as opponents rather than teammates. When life rushes in and divides couples, there cannot be any real success in the union. There will only be war within and war without. A house divided against itself cannot stand.

I cannot count how many times I've coached married women and couples, and advised with them while I pastored with my husband. So many of them were at odds over small things, but used language toward each other that some enemies wouldn't use. They shared a home, bills and responsibilities, and a bed, but they didn't share respect and real love. Love, you see, does not destroy or tear down, but couples tear each other down all the time because of a moment of anger, frustration or misunderstanding.

When we attack our mates verbally, physically or emotionally, we are in essence roughing the passer. We are attacking our star player. We're basically attacking ourselves because we are united in commitment to our mates. To tear down the person you love is to tear yourself down. If your teammate is broken, more of the burden to carry the relationship or team falls upon you. It's self-destructive.

Chapter 8

No Huddle

The pace of life can pick up without warning just like in football when they have a no huddle play. The thing I love about football is the flexibility of calling audibles and changing plays at a moment's notice. When the offensive team catches a good play that gets past the defense, they may come with a hurry up repeat play, not allowing for a huddle. So much like life.

My son used to be a Madden football fan. Sometimes, he had no one else to play with him so I'd try to play the game even though I didn't really understand most of the plays. I would randomly choose a defensive play, and the only offensive plays I understood were the streaks, my favorite being Hail Mary. Every now and again, I accidently replayed my last play without a huddle and finally figured out how to use that to work on my behalf. It was rare for me to have a successful play so when I did hit a streak of luck, I'd wear it out. I could usually get at least two good runs or passes from a no huddle before I had to change plays. In life, things are no different.

Sometimes, you don't have time to regroup. It's as if life is forcing no huddles. You have to make the best out of the hand you were dealt. You have to stay alert and make adjustments without seeking everyone else's approval.

No Regroups

During a particularly hard time in my life, I was battling tachycardia and high blood pressure. Then came the Rocky Mountain Spotted Fever I got during my travels promoting *The Rape of Innocence: Taking Captivity Captive*. Illness was knocking me on my butt left and right. I wasn't prepared to be sick. I wasn't prepared to be disabled. I was newly married at that time and if you can believe it, I felt so guilty for getting sick right after the wedding. It felt like I'd robbed the man of a full, happy, productive life. And sure enough, I saw my illnesses suck the life right out of him, along with draining every dime we could make. I didn't know what to do.

As I dealt with my illnesses, I also tried to keep my business growing and do as much for myself as possible. But then came Lupus and seizures. Before I could gather my wits, I was being hit with something else. It was an all-out blitz. Eventually, it worked and my husband and I split up. We had been found lacking. There was no time for a regroup. No time to sit down and formulate a plan to overcome the attacks on our marriage. It was no huddle and so we had to think on our feet.

In any relationship, things will not always be tulips and daisies. Sometimes, you go through things that no one expected or possibly plan for. But when you commit to thinking on your feet and thinking together, you get through it. It's all about teamwork, as in the game of football.

The quarterback is super important, but so is every other player in their given field. A QB is amazing in his role, but he may suck as a tight end. A wide receiver that can bring that ball in and run it for a touchdown is priceless. But he will only shine as a wide receiver. He may be a disaster in the role of kicker. Thus, a team is about each party being in the right position and perfecting the position they hold.

In relationships, two people agree to bond together as a single entity. They must learn how to love and build one another, and commit to doing so daily. The woman is not more important than the man nor is the man more important than the woman. They are one. They must survive all obstacles as one.

When things go sideways in a hurry, the wise must learn not to blame or make an opponent out of a teammate. Who has time for blame when there is a war raging without? You have bills due, responsibilities, personal and professional goals, children to raise and more. The world is not set up to be friendly or sympathetic, or to give you a hand out toward success and peace. You have to command it. You have to stand and possess it anyway.

When couples fight and argue and demolish one another, they are also pushing each other backwards. They become like the quarterback who is trying to get away from the pressure, running backwards, looking for an opening to put the ball in. The QB cannot ground the ball, intentional grounding, because that is a penalty. If he throws it at the wrong time in the wrong direction, it could lead to an interception. If he gets tackled as he is running back, the next down will require additional yards that must be made up. In the pros, like in life, the pressure is real!

Chapter 9

Field Goal Attempts

There are a few ways to score in football. When a QB sees that his chances of a touchdown are slim to none, and his offensive team is worn out, often times instead of another run, the team will opt for a field goal attempt. It is still live play and the defensive team is going to try to stop it, but sometimes, that is a team's best hope of a score rather than gambling for the big score of a TD. Sometimes it works, even at astronomical distances. Other times it doesn't, even if the team is quite close.

Earlier in the book, I talked to you about the blitz. If the blitz is the pressure of the game, the field goal is the release valve. It can add to the score of the team and salvage a round of bad plays. From the defensive end, they were able to prevent THE score, the touchdown. So it is something of a comfortable medium for two teams with very opposite agendas. I bet by now, you already know where I'm going with this.

Have you ever shared a bed with someone, maybe even a pillow, but didn't know what they were thinking, how they were feeling, or where they were going? Have you looked into someone's eyes and said, "I love you" while wondering who they really were? It's likely that you said yes to both of those questions.

In relationships, terrible atrocities are done daily. There is the woman who has a husband who would gladly die for her, but she spends her energy trying to attract other men. There is the man, who after going through hell to find and win the heart of a loyal wife, now finds himself paying other women money to entertain his lustful desires. There are people who can look their mates straight to the eye and swear their undying love with the smell of another person still on their bodies. Yes, on the down and dirty side of life, the heart is gambled away, abused, stepped on and kicked because of games. The casualties are high on both sides of the field. No one is winning and no one can win this war.

Some call it the war of the sexes, but by any name, it often damages all parties. You see, we've been talking about football, but we're also talking relationships. Relationships require the parties to relate. We are in essence in war with someone and calling it a relationship, but nothing could be further from the truth.

Men often say they want loyalty and honor from their wives. But if they do not themselves interject loyalty and honor, then they dishonor themselves by not providing the same that is being required.

Women often say they want fidelity and security from their husbands. But if they fail to be those things, how can they know when they've found them?

So now, we have everyone with high expectations and low investments. They are expecting an unreasonable return on what has been injected into the relationship. Men and women meet, attraction comes, and then almost immediately, they pit themselves in opposition to one another, each blindly trying to outflank the other so that they can get what they want without exposing their hand. Talk about a dog eat dog world.

After a few failed attempts at getting it without giving any of it up, the name of the football game, a lot of people begin to look for a comfortable medium. They are willing to concede a little of this to get a little of that. It is that age old idea of compromise. But not always is compromise a good thing. Let me first use football to show you how.

When a team that is behind a considerable amount manages to get a field goal, no one is upset or worried, especially if it happens late in the game. However, if a team that was behind lands a field goal that puts them up a point or two, the defensive team, while glad it wasn't a touchdown, is still now the defensive team that lost their team the leading score. So while it isn't the worst thing that could have happened, it still can be a very dangerous thing. I've seen many football games won by field goals. So then, it only benefits the one who adds the score, even if it is a small score.

In a relationship when compromises come down, if they are one side too often, it causes a shift that adds a measure of control to the one who is conceding less. If you gave up school to be with him, gave up friends to be with her, gave up opportunities to appease a mate, then you are yet losing ground. The compromise you have chosen is causing a war within you. It puts you in a losing situation because now you are being untrue to yourself, and thus untrue to the relationship. So then, that compromise, instead of becoming the glue that binds you and your mate together, becomes the mortar in a wall that is being constructed between you two.

You see, the truth is, for every defensive team in the football world, if there is any score for the opposing team, they have failed at their primary job, stopping a score. Every failure puts more pressure on their offense, and jeopardizes their ability to win the game. But when a team is in the thick of it, barely holding on, a field goal by the opposing side can seem like a blessing or a favor. Wow! Can you see that correlation?

When you've been in the thick of it so long, fiery love trial after another, even a field goal at your expense seems like a favorable outcome. I remember listening to some player interviews. I've literally heard players from the losing team say things like, "At least they didn't blow us out." Can you believe that? But aren't we guilty of that exact behavior in relationships?

You see, once upon a time, you didn't want infidelity, deception and laziness. Then, after going through that and some more stuff, you find yourself saying, "If I could just find a man who came home every night…" or "If only I had a woman who can help on the bills a little…" We make all sorts of concessions for the sake of not being alone, just to end up in a relationship and feel more alone than ever due to compromising what should never be compromised, our hearts.

When It Counts - Play

There is another time when a field goal is attempted, after the touchdown. It is worth less because you are set up in the striking zone. So instead of 3 points, it is worth only 1 point, but a miss isn't common in the NFL. Most kickers can kick a field goal after touchdown in their sleeps… except for the few who have missed it for one reason or another. Times like that are almost newsworthy events. Why? Because a professional kicker is supposed to be able to do that with relative ease. Even the announcers treat the field goals as if they have already happened when they see the team setting up for one. It's laughable.

The compromise we spoke about earlier was during the relationship. Well, you can look at the field goal after touchdown as compromise after marriage. That's a great time to compromise, though you still must learn how not to betray yourself while trying to honor someone else, even your husband or wife.

Compromise after marriage can seem to yield less immediate results than a compromise before marriage. The fanfare is often not there. In fact, your sacrifice may seem to go unnoticed. But compromise after marriage is just a part of the game and it makes for a more harmonious relationship.

A touchdown without a field goal seems odd, like somehow something went missing. Oh, I'm always excited when the team decides to go for the two point conversion. It adds flavor to the game. But without that customary field goal, it feels like watching a familiar dance but having a crucial part omitted.

I call a field goal a "when it counts" play. It can win football games. Likewise, compromise can salvage a marriage, so long as balance is kept as the couple seeks to find a place of common ground.

Chapter 10

The Chosen 11

In football, the offensive and defensive teams both have 11 players on the field during game play. Now, don't jump to conclusions thinking I'm about to give you permission to go find some extra help. Ha! No. We're going to look at the process of choosing these 11 starters.

Remember earlier, we discussed coaching strategies. Well, here's where that comes into play again. For some coaches, they want to warm their star players up with some game time. For others, they want to save them for when it counts. Thus, the team on the field at the beginning of the game may or may not be the best the team has to offer. Outsiders can never tell without taking a look at some player statistics. But the coach knows. He knows why he selected those chosen 11 who begin the game.

While writing this book, I began doing a lot of coaching with single, successful women. And because I now date a little, I had the pleasure of meeting some very balanced and successful gentlemen. I don't think I meant it to turn into research for a book, but I find myself probing those who are actively seeking love. I want to know what they are looking for if there are no holds barred. If they could design a mate from scratch, what would the characteristics be?

Likewise, I'm always questioning couples who have been married 10, 20, and 30 years. What characteristics kept them together? What did they do to survive the onslaught of outer distractions and inner doubts?

For the first time, I want to discuss the chosen 11 virtues that will lead the team to victory every single time.

1. Courage

No journey is partaken without courage. No great or small work begins without first someone gathering the courage to make an attempt. Courage is not the absence of fear or doubt. Courage is not supreme confidence in self. Courage is the ability to do what needs to be done even if your heart is trembling. Even the most courageous often stand with their knees knocking. The point being that they stand anyway.

In football, courage is what makes the team suit up, never knowing what a game could bring, even potentially broken bones. Still, they suit up and go out to play.

In relationships, it takes courage to make your desires known to one another. It takes courage to choose each other daily even as you discover things about one another you don't care for. It takes courage to start a relationship and courage to stay in it.

2. Integrity

Okay, I'll be the first to admit that integrity is one of those words that gets thrown around a lot. It just sounds like something a politician would use to sway voters. However, integrity is still one of the cornerstones of human to human relations. And it is an absolute necessity amongst those who hope to build an intimate relationship.

In football, integrity is what makes a player pull back from causing unnecessary injury to someone on the opposing team. It is what helps a player take the well-deserved foul calls without pitching a fit. Integrity keeps players and refs from cheating.

It doesn't function much differently in relationships. Integrity refuses to deceive or manipulate. Integrity is putting all the cards on the table and asking for what is desired while presenting what is being offered. It is necessary for the survival of a relationship and particularly a marriage.

3. Vision

Vision is not the same as sight. Most people can see. But not all seeing people have vision. Vision comes from an inner eye that is attached to a made up mind about something. Vision is about having direction for life. Where are you going? What's your destination?

In football, the vision is far beyond the game being played. Every team dreams of the Super Bowl. In relationships, most of the time things are not as clear.

Most women have the fantasy of marriage and the white picket fence hard wired into their DNA. For men, some envision building an empire with their mate while others only want to build a family. It doesn't much matter what your vision is so long as you have one. The Bible records at Proverbs 29:18 that without vision, the people perish.

4. *Passion*

You could define passion as an inner burning desire that has the power to drive you. Passion isn't just the burning desire to know each other sexually, but also the drive to build a life together. Not everything happens in the bedroom, but for everything, you both must have passion.

Football is a dangerous and painful sport. Even a good day in football yields some sprains and tenderness. To continue playing a game that hurts, you need to be passionate about the game itself.

Relationships are also dangerous in that another person has the ability to hurt you emotionally. Relationships can be painful, even when they are good. Therefore, without a passion for life, for the institution of marriage, for coupling, no relationship can last. Passion has to burn and the goal should be to make it burn brighter with each passing day.

5. *Fidelity*

Most people would have used the word "loyalty" in place of fidelity. But loyalty falls a little shy of the point I'm trying to make.

Fidelity is faithfulness in face of opposition, loyalty and unwavering support. Fidelity has to be a characteristic each party brings to the table. Life gives us plenty of opportunities to be an infidel. To maintain your relationships in life, you must not only take a stand for the team you fight for, the beliefs you hold and the people you love, but you must *also* be ready with unwavering support.

Once upon a time in football, teams were pretty much set. There was no free agency. But in 1992, modern free agency began that allowed teams to make themselves over and over and over again, making deals to bring in more talent sooner. Now everyone has their opinions and for some, free agency is the best thing that happened to the game. Personally, not that I'm an avid fan or understand every aspect of football, but free agency seems to ruin the heart of the sport- a team growing together and learning to play better. In this new system, the superstars are greatly rewarded and those who don't develop as quickly are often pushed to the back and eventually out of the game. Now, superstardom is encouraged, and the team is often left to suffer when their best players are sent off to other teams that pay more money.

Whether in football or life, fidelity is the difference between building self or building the team. Fidelity sticks in it for the team, knowing that there is no way to grow the team without growing with it. Every team owner hopes for a great player with fidelity, someone who won't give up on the team. Isn't that also what we desire in a meaningful relationship?

6. *Communication*

How can any team or entity involving more than one person actually survive or function without some method of communication? Even the human body communicates with itself via nerves and the brain. Most certainly, a team as well as a relationship, must learn to effectively communicate.

Not all communication is verbal. For instance, in most professional sports, there are signs and signals given to relay a message between teammates. Likewise in relationships, couples communicate via body language and maybe even planned code.

The problems begin where communication breaks down. In a team setting, if the receiver does not carefully observe his quarterback, they can easily miscommunicate and miss scoring opportunities. Likewise in a relationship, failure to communicate will cause couples to miss opportunities to grow in all aspects.

7. Humility

Some people end up with low self-esteem aiming at humility, not understanding this characteristic at all. Humility is keeping yourself in proper perspective. I remember looking it up one day and it said something about placing low importance on yourself. I hate that definition because humility doesn't mean you are unimportant or unassertive. Humility is not placing yourself above others either.

In football, each person has their own role to play. They should never minimize the importance of that role or themselves in that role. In relationships, neither should either party feel the need to debase or lower themselves for one another. That isn't how a team or partnership is built.

Through humility, each person maximizes their own role and potential in that role. They stay their course and in their own lane. No role is of elevated importance but each is different and purposeful.

8. Generosity

So I know you're probably thinking, "I want to see her use generosity and football in the same sentence." Ha. I know. I had to sit with it for a moment before it hit me.

Generous can mean unselfish and kind, yet also abundant. It can be defined as giving plenty or having plenty. Generous is a word that covers both sides of abundance. It paints a vivid picture that a giver increases in value and substance.

I love when fellow football players celebrate one another. They edify one another. During various interviews, some players even acknowledge the skill and amazing talent of an opponent. That's the spirit of generosity. Giving praise and accolades to others when they are deserved.

Generosity is how relationships survive the hard times. It puts each person in the attitude of a giver and so no one is counting what's received. Only what's given. What an amazing environment for a relationship!

9. Determination

Every person has a dream, some seemingly more difficult than others. But there is a chasm between dreamers and achievers. It's called determination.

Every player on the football team has to decide they will play the game to the best of their ability. At kickoff, everyone is fresh and ready. But as game time passes, weariness can begin to sit in. At that point, it is all an inside job. It is a matter of determination to keep working for the goal.

Determination takes you where emotions cannot. Determination is how couples stick together through tough events. Even the best relationships have periods of testing and trials. But when two people determine to work together toward a common end, nothing is impossible.

Every player must be determined if the team is to succeed. Likewise, each party in a relationship must be determined to stay in it for it to work.

10. Flexibility

Contrary to popular opinion, the ability to bend is a highly desirable trait in every field, and especially in football and relationships.

Bo Jackson was one of the most amazing athletes of his time. He played professional football and baseball and was named in All Star in both sports, the only athlete to ever do so. He had multiple talents that made him rich and led to ESPN naming him one of the greatest athletes of all time. He was flexible and easily molded when it came to sports.

Most people have an idea of what kind of life and relationship they want. The problems come when what they have and what they want are not the same. When you're inflexible, you can give up on something amazing with all the potential in the world because it is not what you thought it should be. But when you're flexible, you adjust to difficulties in life and relationships without abandoning others or feeling bitter because of the difficulties.

No matter what you do in life, there is going to be some disappointments. Not everything will go according to your plan. That, however, does not mean you should just ship. Now in my case, I needed to jump ship. However, because I was rigid and inflexible, I stayed stuck in a bad situation for much too long. Inflexibility has that double whammy effect: it can make you give up the right things or stick too tightly to the wrong things. However, when you choose to be flexible, you choose to stay open to processing new information, which can help you make the best decisions in your life and relationships.

A QB has to be flexible because what he wants to do may not be an option. That isn't known until the ball is hiked. In life, you don't know what a day will hold, but flexibility keeps you ready.

11. Self-Control

There is absolutely nothing worthwhile you can do when you lack control. Players are ejected from games all the time because they have terrible temper tantrums. They play angry and aggressive, but cannot tolerate being called on it.

Self-control is the ability to manage your emotions and actions so that you are not driven by circumstances to do things you should not do. During my time as a pastor, I once counseled a woman whose husband was critically injured within the first year of their young marriage. She said for many years, she remained faithful. She took her vows seriously. He lived 18 years after the accident and she had the testimony of remaining true though he was financially and sexually debilitated because of his physical condition. I thought that was probably one of the best testimonies I heard. And I asked her how she did it. She responded self-control.

In professional sports, you cannot allow being in a losing position make you cheat. Same in life. There'll always be the temptation to do the wrong things, say the wrong things, think the wrong things. But self-control helps you not yield to that temptation. Is it easy? Not always. It's not popular either. But it is powerful and puts you worlds ahead on the road to good relationships.

Epilogue

During the 2010 playoffs between the Saints and the Vikings, Brett Favres' last dance, the viciousness of the game was obvious. I watched as Favre was hit repeatedly, injured and the referees did nothing. It was so bad that even after the game, an investigation was launched. Come to find out, the Saints were actually trying to injure Viking players and particularly Brett Favre. But the most tragic part of the story is the Saints won that game and no amount of fines or penalties could change the outcome.

In my relationship, I was cheated on repeatedly. But I stayed in the game because I was afraid not to. I had a thousand reasons come to mind for holding on to something I knew wasn't good for me. But it wasn't until I learned my own value, took a look at myself and committed to doing what needed to be done that change occurred.

This book is not to tell you which relationships to stay in or leave. This book is about looking at unhealthy relationships in general and how they destroy our lives. Isn't it funny how someone can grab a live wire and become unable to drop it until they have been fried? Maybe that is exactly what you're doing holding on to the person who is causing you the most damage.

Like my beloved Brett Favre, eventually there comes a time to let it go, the game. There comes a time to retire. Dan Marino retired. Bo Jackson retired. No one should play the game forever. And in relationships, you shouldn't have to play games and endure godless injury to your heart. But you've been waiting on others to acknowledge that and spare you. But this is a spare you must pick up yourself. It is your job to protect your heart. It is your responsibility to ensure that no one is allowed to trespass and destroy your life. It's up to you to call it quits.

One of the most amazing things happened to me when I decided I was done with games and bad relationships. Actually it was two things: I discovered my own worth and what I bring to the table, and I met people who enriched my life in ways I still cannot fully describe. To you, what you know and your surroundings is all there is, but whether you believe it, there is another world out there. You cannot see it or participate in it while holding on to the one you are in right now. You cannot fathom men who don't lie or cheat, or women who don't manipulate and complain. You cannot fathom relationships that grow better, sweeter and deeper by the day because you've never seen it. I was the same way until I walked out of the darkness.

Light illuminates your path. And your heart is supposed to be full of light. But if you keep subjecting it to abuse, it turns hard, cold and dark. I say to you today, follow light. Don't allow anyone to put your lights out, to darken or harden your heart. Not everything is a game, and your love life is for sure not to be toyed with. If you take nothing else from this book, I leave you with this sentence: you can do and have better.

www.ingramcontent.com/pod-product-compliance
Lightning Source LLC
LaVergne TN
LVHW051151080426
835508LV00021B/2588